To Shilpa,
I hope this book bless...
Thank you for your ...
Lots of love,
Naomi xx
22/05/22

Deep Calls Unto Deep, Wisdom from the Heart

© 2022 Naomi Rae Wharton

Published by Rae of Sunshine

Designed by Naomi Rae Wharton

Edited by Hannah Williams

ISBN: 978-1-3999-2310-1

All rights reserved. No part of this publication may be reproduced, distributed, or transmitted in any form or by any means, including photocopying, recording, or other electronic or mechanical methods, without the prior written permission of the publisher, except in the case brief quotations embodied in critical reviews and certain other noncommercial uses permitted by copyright law.

Scriptures are taken from the King James Version Bible (KJV) and New King James Version Bible (NKJV).

First printing edition 2022
Printed in the UK

www.raeofsunshine.uk

Wisdom from the Heart

31 DAY DEVOTIONAL

NAOMI RAE WHARTON

To my beautiful family, friends and the community of Rae of Sunshine; thank you for your continual love and support.

I hope this book blesses you and all those that come into contact with it near and far.

Love and light,
Naomi Rae x

*Deep calls unto deep
at the noise of Your waterfalls;
All Your waves and billows
have gone over me.*
Psalm 42:7 (NKJV)

CONTENTS

Introduction 14

A Call for Courage 19
A Childlike Faith 21
A Turbulent Triumph 23
Be Bold 27
Blind Spot 29
Character Building 33
Death by Deceit 37
Faith in the Midst of Fear 41
Growing Pains 43
Hall of Faith 47
Heart Work 49
Heavenly Dining on an Earthly Platter 53
Help Above 55
Identity Theft 57
Let the Spirit Win 59
Love Languages 61
Melodies From Heaven 65

Nature, Nurture and Nourishment 67
No Shame in the Shadows............................... 69
Rough Side of the Mountain 71
Search the Scriptures..................................... 73
Serve Your Testimony 77
Smarter than We Act...................................... 79
Spiritual Senses 83
The Grave is a Standard Size............................ 87
The Ultimate Key... 91
The Uncomfortable, Unexpected and Uncertainty... 93
We are God's Masterpiece 95
What Has Luck Got to do With It?...................... 97
Wisdom Has no Age Restriction 99
You and Yahweh 101

Introduction

The deep.

The place where a lot of people fear to go. The fear of the unknown. The reality of circumstances. The vulnerability of oneself.

But how can we truly discover the depths of our souls, the depths of our true authentic self without launching into the deep.

Wisdom is depth and depth is substance like a body of water.

Psalm 42, is an expression of a man's unbearable circumstances. In the midst of depression and despair he knows where his hope can be found - in God. Even though the presence of God is questioned, God's faithfulness is not and the man's hope lies in the deep.

As I share my testimony in this introduction, I hope you understand the depths of why I write, how God speaks to me and why I'm a strong advocate for mental wellbeing.

VALLEY TO VICTORY
(Trigger warning)

Enough was enough! I packed my bag and left. Little did I know, I was about to embark on my last journey, go on my last walk, have my last meal and take my last breath.

It was December 2017, a few days before Christmas. I was alone in a hotel room, sitting on the bed in my blue cozy pyjamas, but my eyes were full of tears. I had a heavy heart and a confused mind. I was in too much agony to function. In that moment I decided to write - my last words. The pain flowed through the pen to the paper – it was filled with I love you's, goodbyes and a justification as to why I didn't belong in the world anymore. All I wanted to do was escape.

I could see an end but there was no light. I scanned the room, there was nothing to assist me in my plans which added a level of frustration.
I don't recall what I did next. I somehow got through the morning and the rest of the day.

I felt like I had the deepest darkest secret that would have literally taken me to the grave. I had to get it out of my system and take a step towards acceptance - that I was suicidal.

This was the lowest I had ever been in my life. I had to seek help.

After that episode, I spent many days feeling tormented. In my mind being at home didn't feel safe, my local park was a death trap, talking to people felt too much but I must admit going to work was a saving grace. It was something productive I could do every day.

My secret was unbearable and I spoke to a close friend, she supported me along with a couple of other people I trusted. I decided to go to the GP to get further help but I refused medication. I was then advised to attend Talking therapies. This was difficult for me and it was the first experience I had with a counsellor and to be honest it wasn't a great one.

Even though work felt like a saving grace at times, some days it was too difficult for me to go into the office. Eventually I got the courage to speak to my line manager and HR about my mental health.

I was able to access Private Health care, get professional help and start my healing process.

Making a choice and being honest were two important factors in the midst of seeking help.

With the help of counselling and psychotherapy, I was on a road of discovery. Digging deep as to how I got there, analysing patterns of behaviour, elements of unhappiness and the root causes.

Anxiety, depression and PTSD were identified. I had no idea how much pain I was carrying. Trauma from childhood took a hold of me and stifled my growth into adulthood. I looked for love in the wrong places and many situations growing up added to the pain.

I had a belief system that I didn't deserve to be happy, but the truth is - that was a lie. We all deserve to be happy. Unfortunately, we can't change what happened to us, but we can heal from it.

Our past is a place of reference not a place of residence.

If it wasn't for counselling, my faith and my support system, I would not be where I am now. I can't stress enough how much life is for living and how much better it feels on the sunny side. I no longer write notes of pain but expressions of purpose, wisdom, encouragement, love and affirmations.

I seek peace, I walk in freedom, and I live in hope.

BLUE OCEAN FLOOR

Quiet as a mouse!
She must be a mute

What they didn't know…
She didn't speak to amuse
Neither to abuse

A conscious speaker full of empathy
They say still waters run deep
And that she is

She embodies a diver
Only the brave can meet her down under

Where hidden pearls are found
And wisdom is released to the surface

Step out in faith.

DEEP CALLS UNTO DEEP

A Call for Courage

Joshua 1:9 (NKJV)
Have I not commanded you? Be strong and of good courage; do not be afraid, nor be dismayed, for the Lord your God is with you wherever you go."

I didn't acknowledge how much of a transition I have had until people in my circle have told me about my progress. It has been beautiful to hear and to feel the love of God through them.

In 2020 I was walking in courage without even realising it. I had done things I never thought I would:
- Climbed a mountain
- Spoken on a radio station
- Cut my hair
...just to name a few. These required perseverance, confidence and faith.

I made a conscious decision to have courage as my word of the year. To step out in faith because I know that God has my back.

I encourage you all to step out in faith. Do all the things you said you were going to do or wanted to do. Even if it has been done before, it doesn't matter because no-one is you! Better yet, what has God called you to do that you are running away from? There is no hiding place.

God is able! He would not call you do something for you to fail. Our God is faithful. I can't express enough how important accountability is. It just takes one person. Speak it into existence, pray and put in the work!

Isaiah 40:31 (NKJV)
But those who wait on the Lord Shall renew their strength; They shall mount up with wings like eagles, They shall run and not be weary, They shall walk and not faint.

Be childlike in love and faith.

A Childlike Faith

To have childlike faith and not be childish. Childlike in the sense of innocence and trust.

Matthew 18:2-4 (NKJV)
² Then Jesus called a little child to Him, set him in the midst of them,
³ [A]nd said, "Assuredly, I say to you, unless you are converted and become as little children, you will by no means enter the kingdom of heaven.
⁴ Therefore whoever humbles himself as this little child is the greatest in the kingdom of heaven.

A child isn't fazed by their surroundings; they do things in faith. They are entrusting towards their parents until they do something that may upset them. They look up to their parents, they love without question.

As adults we are influenced by surroundings, opinions etc.
But we have a duty onto our spiritual calling and heavenly Father to come humbly and be in adoration, for He has done no wrong and will do no harm, and gives us an unconditional love like no other. Be encouraged to look onto your heavenly Father as a child would do theirs.

Their hero!

The essence of God's sweet, unconditional love is everywhere.
There is more than enough love to go around, and it amazes me.

Be childlike in love and faith.

Purpose
Patience
Pursuit

A Turbulent Triumph

How can a triumph be turbulent?

Purpose
An analogy of the church:
God gave me an analogy and visualisation of the church within the aviation industry. That churches, are planes going to a destination and the workers are the ministers. In order for a plane to fly, there needs to be a pilot, co-pilot, flight crew, cabin crew, navigator.

- Flight attendants have different roles to fulfill. They can't one day be attending to passengers and then the next try and fly the plane. So, it is in the church, we have purpose, and we can't fulfill a position we haven't been called to do.
- We are constantly in training mode even when we have been called – we must maintain a teachable spirit.
- We are not always in the same place at the same time.
- No role is more important than the other, from the usher to the Bishop.
- God is our ultimate navigator, ensuring that we are aiming for the correct runway and have a smooth landing.

Psalm 57:2 (NKJV)
I will cry out to God Most High, To God who performs all things for me.

Patience
Patience during turbulent times.

What is turbulence? What causes turbulence?

[*Turbulence is just some sort of change in the air around your plane. Air isn't nothingness; it's a fluid, like water. Currents of air move up and down, ripple out, change direction, and change speed.*

Some of the things that cause turbulence are easier to predict. Thunderstorms push air up and down, so your pilot will use weather reports and instruments on the plane to avoid the worst of the storm. The movement of air as it's warmed by the sun causes turbulence. Changes in weather are another cause of turbulence. Mountains and other geographic structures cause turbulence when air moves up or down, and that ripple effect can last a long time.

Airplanes themselves disturb the air and can cause turbulence for the flight behind them, which is one of the reasons air traffic controllers give airplanes a lot of space (and why you might have to wait to take off). And the air near the jet streams that wrap around our planet can be turbulent even though the skies look clear; this is called "clear air turbulence."

The most important thing to know is that turbulence isn't dangerous. It might be a bit uncomfortable, but your plane is built to handle the worst. ~ Canadian Mental Health Association (https://cmha.bc.ca/documents/what-is-turbulence)]

In this description the phrase that stood out to me was ***Airplanes themselves disturb the air and can cause turbulence for the flight behind them.***

This reminds of the impact that the church has in shifting atmospheres within and around them. The importance of unity, resilience and faith that is required in all seasons.

We may feel like we have endured many seasons for a long period of time but it's in these turbulent times we can truly exercise patience. The atmosphere is worth being shaken for growth, for healing, for the next generation.

Psalm 37:7-9 (NKJV)
[7] Rest in the Lord and wait patiently for Him; Do not fret because of him who prospers in his way, Because of the man who brings wicked schemes to pass.
[8] Cease from anger and forsake wrath; Do not fret—it only causes harm.
[9] For evildoers shall be [b]cut off; But those who wait on the Lord, They shall inherit the earth.

Pursuit
To truly pursue God is to allow God to have his way and seek his righteousness. Allowing Gods plan to reign. Gods will not our will. God navigates, God orders our steps. His word is sure.

Having lack of obedience will cause our planes to go in all sorts of directions, so we must be attentive to his voice, discern in the midst of storms, be accepting of change and allow God to mould our character and be blessed with a spiritual 20:20 vision.

Psalm 34:14 (NKJV)
Depart from evil and do good; Seek peace and pursue it.

Whether you're in training mode or flight mode, despite what may seem like evil is triumphant - God is in is in the midst, God is in control.

I pray that whatever you need to declare you will do so unto the Lord. If there is any unwanted baggage, excess baggage that causes you to pay an extra price for – let it go and may your load be lighter as you land in Gods promise. May you obtain the joy, peace and love of God.

Be bold with your life!

Be Bold

I encourage you to be bold and stand in your truth.

Make bold statements and affirm yourself with the Word. Don't sit on your testimonies and victories – someone needs to hear them and know that there is a hope. We all have a story to tell and we all have something to celebrate and for that we give God thanks.

Be bold with your life!

Every season was necessary; the hurts, the pains were necessary. Your tears were not in vain.

We give thanks that we don't look like what we've been through and even as we are tried and tested in this season it will not be in vain as we become stronger, wiser and better.

Deuteronomy 31:6 (NKJV)
Be strong and of good courage, do not fear nor be afraid of them; for the Lord your God, He is the One who goes with you. He will not leave you nor forsake you."

1 Corinthians 16:13-14 (NKJV)
[13] Watch, stand fast in the faith, be brave, be strong. [14] Let all that you do be done with love.

God is preparing us for something greater that will require a new-found boldness.

God will send people to check our blind spot for us.

Blind Spot

When driving they say check your blind spot. *Why?* Because there are certain things you can't see out your mirrors. Extra observation is required.

In leadership they use a technique called the 'Johari window' to better understand relationships with themselves and others. And one of the four panes is called the blind spot.

Unknown to yourself, known to others.

Some occasions we can see for ourselves and other times we can't.

God will send people to check our blind spot for us. It allows us to see a perspective we haven't considered because we simply could not see it. They may highlight a characteristic we thought we never had, or something we dislike and try to suppress, but we must check ourselves.
It's not always the other person, so look within – *what are you doing? What fruit are you bearing? What are you lacking?*

Proverbs 12:15 (NKJV)
The way of a fool is right in his own eyes, But he who heeds counsel is wise.

Receive good counsel and don't dismiss. What your present self is being protected from now, will help your future self. The wisdom you digest now will be embedded in your heart for future reference.

God will also send his angels. We are always being watched over.
When we can't see what's around the corner, GOD CAN!

Psalm 91:11-12 (NKJV)
[11] For He shall give His angels charge over you, To keep you in all your ways.

[12] In their hands they shall bear you up, Lest you dash your foot against a stone.

Don't forget to check your blind spot before you move!

THE JOHARI WINDOW

	Known to self	Unknown to self
Known to others	**OPEN** — Things that you and everyone else know	**BLIND** — Things that you are unaware of but others know
Unknown to others	**HIDDEN** — Things that are known by you but unknown to others	**UNKNOWN** — Things that are unknown by you and everyone else

DEEP CALLS UNTO DEEP

Keep going!

Character Building

One evening I was on my way home from work and God dropped character building in my spirit and the word 'resilience' was repeating over and over.

Resilience:
the capacity to recover quickly from difficulties; toughness.

I believe this is a mighty characteristic that we all obtain but don't always acknowledge and give thanks for.

We are STRONG!

This life is hard, and God said narrow is the way, but we can do all things in Christ that strengthens us.

Romans 5:3-5 (NKJV)
[3] And not only that, but we also glory in tribulations, knowing that tribulation produces perseverance; [4] [A]nd perseverance, character; and character, hope. [5] Now hope does not disappoint, because the love of God has been poured out in our hearts by the Holy Spirit who was given to us.

We are tested on a day-to-day basis. We are faced with adversity time to time but we get back up.

Whether it be a negative word spoken, a financial setback, health issue, broken heart, someone who may have betrayed us, whatever it may be, we get back up.

We keep it moving, as life keeps moving! God has so much in store for us. Keep going! Don't get so consumed by life!

Of course, it's not always likely that we will bounce back as quick as we would like but it's not forever.

Do not stay in a place of wallowing. We are encouraged to fight the good fight of faith.

Our help comes from the Lord.
Reflect on Psalm 121:1-8.

Carry your character of resilience with boldness as we are overcomers.

DEEP CALLS UNTO DEEP

God's ways will always be better!

Death by Deceit

I recall having a particular dream, it wasn't vivid – they never are but I remember people, objects and vague locations.

In this dream was my sister, some friends and I. We went out to eat at a restaurant and they seated us quite close to the door. We were talking, ordered food, etc.

Where we were seated on one side was a small table across the wall that was in arms' reach. Something caught my sister's eye on the table and she pulled out a leaflet.

It was a leaflet for another restaurant. It gave the impression that they had ordered from there and served the food.

Not sure where this went, or if we confronted the restaurant.

But from this God showed me that things are not always presented how we want them to look. Our blessings are not always packaged in a way that we would like or expect.

God will orchestrate things in such a way that may baffle you, but we give thanks.

Isaiah 55:8-9 (NKJV)

[8] "For My thoughts are not your thoughts, Nor are your ways My ways," says the Lord. [9] "For as the heavens are higher than the earth, So are My ways higher than your ways, And My thoughts than your thoughts."

God's way will always be better!

Deception is one of the things that God hates.

In the Book of Psalms there is a plea to God for protection from deceitful mouths.

Psalm 120:2 (NKJV)
Deliver my soul, O Lord, from lying lips And from a deceitful tongue.

Proverbs 12:22 (NKJV)
Lying lips are an abomination to the Lord, But those who deal truthfully are His delight.

Deception is around us day-to-day; therefore the spirit of discernment must be stirred up in order to remain on guard.

Let's be wise and be an army of not just good words but deeds.

Allow faith to counteract fear.

Faith in the Midst of Fear

Psalm 23:4 (NKJV)
Yea, though I walk through the valley of the shadow of death, I will fear no evil; For You are with me; Your rod and Your staff, they comfort me.

Fear is a massive factor in why we fall or seem like we're a failure. Fear cripples us. Even with the feeling of fear, faith can be present.

Fear = Feeling
Faith = Action

If God has revealed something to you or asked you to do something, you may have an instant feeling of fear, but in the midst of that is faith.

If you feel vulnerable, do it anyway
If you're scared do it anyway
If you feel like you're going to be judged, do it anyway and God will deal with them.

Don't do it anyhow but do it anyway.

God is with us and His promises are sure. Have the faith that God is forever present. Don't do it without God.

Allow faith to counteract fear.

Philippians 4:13 (NKJV)
I can do all things through Christ who strengthens me.

It takes time!

Growing Pains

Growing...

Stretches
Hurts
Doesn't always feel good
Doesn't always look pretty

When a child/teenager goes through puberty, it's not always pretty.
Acne, body hair, body sweat, breast growth, genital growth, menstrual cycle etc.
Who likes to be sweaty? Who likes to have hair in certain places that we always seem to get rid of?

No-one!
But it's a part of growth. A teenager's body is prepared for reproduction and becoming an adult. Growing may look ugly but it's just a season.

But growing is..
Necessary
A process
A journey
Life!

An indication of being alive!
One day I was at home on the balcony, and I asked my mum why her plant looked the way it did. It looked weird to me and didn't seem to bloom as it 'should'.

Then when I looked another time, it looked different. It had new growth! My perception was about the current state of the plant and not what it would turn into.

Flowers bloom... We bloom.
It takes time!

Sometimes it may seem like our growth is slow, or has been stunted. But you're still growing! You're still moving! God is working in the background nurturing.

We just have to be patient, because the Word says...

Job 8:7 (NKJV)
Though your beginning was small, Yet your latter end would increase abundantly.

Your latter is greater and your best days are ahead of you.
Preparation for manifestation!

Remember it takes time!

Shine your light in a dark place.

Hall of Faith

*Which scriptures and Biblical affirmations have you inscribed on the stars located in your '**Hall of Faith**'?*

Hebrews 11 is known as this title and we can gain a lot from this scripture.

Hebrews 11:1-3 (NKJV)

[1]. Now faith is the substance of things hoped for, the evidence of things not seen. [2]. For by it the elders obtained a good testimony. [3]. By faith we understand that the worlds were framed by the word of God, so that the things which are seen were not made of things which are visible.

Use your Hall of Faith as a reminder of your resilience, how you've built up your faith, when you fell and how you got up. Take note of the things you do or used to do that helped your faith grow.

There will be a few missing stars along the way but take the leap of faith. As you walk along, retain what God is saying to you and inscribe the wisdom you receive and the whispers of your heart.

Shine your light in a dark place.

We have the tools to maintain a well-kept garden of life.

Heart Work

When was the last time you did some heart work?
Have you dealt with your deep issues?
What are you still hurting from?

Our heart is the centre of us spiritually and physically.

Proverbs 4:23 (NKJV)
Keep your heart with all diligence, For out of it spring the issues of life.

Is your spiritual heart pumping Jesus?
Are you breathing in the Holy Spirit?
Do you feel spiritually alive?

I encourage you to search your hearts. Sometimes it may feel like it's better to hold on than to let go. But true healing arrives when you let go.

May we create a beautiful garden in our hearts that God can dwell in, that He will be well pleased. Well pleased with the fruit that we are bearing on our trees.

The fruit of the spirit:
Galatians 5:22-26 (NKJV)
[22]. But the fruit of the Spirit is love, joy, peace, longsuffering, kindness, goodness, faithfulness,
[23]. [G]entleness, self-control. Against such there is no law.
[24]. And those who are Christ's have crucified the flesh with its passions and desires.
[25]. If we live in the Spirit, let us also walk in the Spirit.
[26]. Let us not become conceited, provoking one another, envying one another.

Plant good seeds and God will nurture them.

Get rid of the weeds - the negative attachments of life that try to weigh us down and overgrow our enriched goodness that God has given.
This life is not for the swift, but God has given us the tools to overcome the strongholds.

We have the tools to maintain a well-kept garden of life.

The Word
Prayer
Holy Spirit
Discernment
Gifts of the spirit
(that we have been blessed with individually – God will reveal)

Just to list a few weedkillers!

We can't always do the work on our own and this is when accountability steps in. The help of your brothers and sisters. We must share the workload. Our gardens of life stretch far and wide. There are a lot of acres to maintain.

There are seasons where we may only be able to maintain the surface level of the weeds and the overgrown plants that we cut down.
But we can't uproot a tree on our own.

Be open to heart work.
Be open to receiving help.
Be honest about what you need to cut down.

We can have heaven on Earth now.

Heavenly Dining on an Earthly Platter

We don't have to wait until the coming of our King and the ascension into heaven to taste and see the glory of God.

We can have heaven on earth now.

God is never far away from us and is very tangible even when we can't see or feel it.

A daily reminder and dose of gratitude can go a long way.
We are blessed and highly favored.
We are not running for our lives.
We can read the Word and speak freely.
We are not being prosecuted.
But we remember those who do not have this privilege and encourage those who we come in contact with.

Romans 14:17 (NKJV)
[F]or the kingdom of God is not eating and drinking, but righteousness and peace and joy in the Holy Spirit.

Life is a blessing and to be **lived.**

What is your piece of heaven today?

God is our help.

Help Above

I remember one morning I woke up unsettled, heavy, upset, angry, and pressed from every side from personal issues to family issues, work, deadlines, emotional stresses, etc.

As I laid in bed with my eyes closed, face up, I saw an opening of light and it turned into a crown.

In this midst of this I was reminded that my help comes from the Lord. Some things are out of our control and we have to give it to God. Our burdens are to be shared and not to be consumed within.

Psalm 121:1-8 (NKJV)
[1] I will lift up my eyes to the hills— From whence comes my help? [2] My help comes from the Lord, Who made heaven and earth. [3] He will not allow your foot to be moved; He who keeps you will not slumber. [4] Behold, He who keeps Israel Shall neither slumber nor sleep. [5] The Lord is your keeper; The Lord is your shade at your right hand. [6] The sun shall not strike you by day, Nor the moon by night. [7] The Lord shall preserve you from all evil; He shall preserve your soul. [8] The Lord shall preserve your going out and your coming in From this time forth, and even forevermore.

The Lord knows the adversity we face and there is 24:7 access to heaven. God also speaks through people. So seek Godly counsel.

Be encouraged knowing that God is our help.

Focus on the now!

Identity Theft

Sometimes we attach ourselves too much to the past and the future. We get so caught up in time that doesn't exist. It has already past or has not yet arrived. The past and future become our identity. This robs us of the most precious time we have.

James 4:14 (NKJV)
[W]hereas you do not know what will happen tomorrow. For what is your life? It is even a vapor that appears for a little time and then vanishes away.

Our life experiences, history, our upbringing is very important. We acknowledge all these things.

It is also very important that we get healing from bad experiences and past traumas. But let's not dwell there, it doesn't exist. You are not who you used to be.

Who are you today?

Focus on the NOW! Today!
Every new day that we are blessed to see becomes a new today.
This is what we have right now – it's tangible.
So is God!

What is God saying to you right now?

Be alert and listen.
Be encouraged that today is the most important time we have.

Your help comes from the Lord.

Let the Spirit Win

Sometimes we lack perseverance, strength or the will to keep pressing on. Yes, we can get weary and frustrated and our minds can run wild, which is natural.

But how often do you let your imagination take control and make up things that are not even real?

When I think unclean or evil thoughts my mind wants it to be removed. I immediately want the Holy Spirit to take reign.

2 Corinthians 10:3-5 (NKJV)
³. For though we walk in the flesh, we do not war according to the flesh.
⁴. For the weapons of our warfare are not carnal but mighty in God for pulling down strongholds,
⁵. [C]asting down arguments and every high thing that exalts itself against the knowledge of God, bringing every thought into captivity to the obedience of Christ[.]

Surrender and allow God to reign. His ways are higher than ours.

Romans 8:13 (NKJV)
For if you live according to the flesh you will die; but if by the Spirit you put to death the deeds of the body, you will live.

At times your flesh may be faithless but the Spirit within you is strengthened by God if you allow Him to. Your help comes from the Lord.

It's all love.

Love Languages

Love is in our bodies, minds and souls.
It's in our breath, our stance, our words but ultimately our actions.
How do we show our love?

It comes in many forms and many languages. Whether it's words of affirmations, quality time, acts of service, receiving gifts or physical touch. It's all love!

If you ask someone if they're ok, how they are; if you remind them of something they're likely to forget, buy a gift, ask if they've been to that appointment they keep on avoiding, give a hug, offer to babysit, cook dinner, do a surprise getaway.

It's all love. Everything is love.

But, what do love languages look like unto God?

Words of affirmation – **Worship**: tell God how much you love and appreciate him. He loves to hear it.

Quality Time – **Meditating on the Word**: God loves to spend time with His children. He wants your attention without distractions. Give God your time.

Gifts – **Giving**: we know God doesn't need our money, but we know it is necessary for the furtherance of his work for His glory and the Kingdom. Trust God with your finances and be a cheerful giver. You'll be blessed.

Acts of service – **Help**: there are many stories and characters that we can learn from in the Bible when it comes to support, sacrifice and sharing. Whether it be helping the homeless, a young person, evangelising or supporting the church, we all have a duty of care.

Physical touch – **Praying**: sometimes we may feel like we can't feel God, but He is there. His presence can be felt. A deep inward vertical connection with God can be achieved through praying. Seek the Holy Spirit for intimacy, a true relationship.

1 John 4:12-13 (NKJV)
[12] No one has seen God at any time. If we love one another, God abides in us, and His love has been perfected in us. [13] By this we know that we abide in Him, and He in us, because He has given us of His Spirit.

What love language will you be practicing in your relationship with God?

ND DEEP CALLS UNTO DEEP

We will always win being on God's team.

Melodies from Heaven

We don't have to stretch too far to have access to heaven. God is right here. We have the Holy Spirit dwelling among us and within us.

Through the Word of God, wisdom, gifts, teachings, praise and much more, we connect with God and one another.

Colossians 3:16 (NKJV)
Let the word of Christ dwell in you richly in all wisdom, teaching and admonishing one another in psalms and hymns and spiritual songs, singing with grace in your hearts to the Lord.

May God shower you with melodies from heaven today and touch your soul in every capacity, that you may be set free and feel a wave of peace and oceans of love from your Heavenly Father.

Let's stay prayed up, support one another, grow in grace and walk in wisdom.

We will always win being on God's team.

God doesn't do things by accident.

Nature, Nurture & Nourishment

Nature – the basic or inherent features, character, or qualities of something
Nurture – care for and protect (someone or something) while they are growing
Nourishment – the food necessary for growth, health, and good condition

As a human race our nature is not always pleasant – the things we do, the things we say, the things we think – but we give God thanks for His grace and nurturing character.

Ephesians 2:8 (NKJV)
For by grace you have been saved through faith, and that not of yourselves; it is the gift of God[.]

Through God's Word and constant nurturing, we are able to grow differently. The conditions that we are planted in may not have been adequate for our development and being uprooted and made uncomfortable was necessary. Changing jobs, losing friends, moving to a new area – God doesn't do things by accident.

In the midst of change how do we maintain our nourishment? We need to meet God halfway and do your part to maintain a healthy spiritual lifestyle. *Are we glowing from the inside out?*

What has been working for you? What has been stunting your growth, successes, and breakthroughs?

Philippians 4:8 (NKJV)
Finally, brethren, whatever things are true, whatever things are noble, whatever things are just, whatever things are pure, whatever things are lovely, whatever things are of good report, if there is any virtue and if there is anything praiseworthy - meditate on these things.

Will you allow God to protect you?

No Shame in the Shadows

To be in the shadows, the shadows under the Almighty, is a hiding place, a sacred place, a safe space.

When we hide in the shadows of our own selves, our inner critic will condemn and bring about shame. There is no solace in this, there is no peace. There is only peace where God resides.

Will you allow God's wings to protect you?

Our Heavenly Father wants you to be the best version of yourself and you can't do that by allowing shame to rule you. This will hold you back from your ambitions and all that God has called you to be.

Don't deprive yourself, your loved ones, the young one that's similar to your younger self. You are blessed and have something to give to your community.

Psalm 91:1-4 (NKJV)
[1] He who dwells in the secret place of the Most High Shall abide under the shadow of the Almighty. [2] I will say of the Lord, "He is my refuge and my fortress; My God, in Him I will trust." [3] Surely He shall deliver you from the snare of the fowler And from the perilous pestilence.
[4] He shall cover you with His feathers, And under His wings you shall take refuge; His truth shall be your shield and buckler.

This scripture is encouragement for how God is our refuge, Prince of peace, divine truth and protector.

Don't stay stuck in your own shadow. Rest in your Saviour's shadow of love.

What is a diamond without pressure?

Rough Side of the Mountain

Mountains symbolise journeys: the rough, the smooth, the peaks, the valleys.

There are rocks that are immovable, unshakable due to the strong foundation and the nature of the materiality of what the mountain is actually made of.

God's foundation is solid, full of love, peace, joy, strength, guidance, salvation, justification, truth and so much more.

What foundation are you standing on?

You may feel like you've been on the rough side for some time, but it will be worth it. The process is worth it. You may slip on a shaky rock but then the next step will be a solid one; you will not fall.

What are you made of?

Isaiah 41:10 (NKJV)
Fear not, for I am with you; Be not dismayed, for I am your God. I will strengthen you, Yes, I will help you, I will uphold you with My righteous right hand.'

Without the suffering there would be no success.
Without the valleys there would be no victory. Without the pressure there would be no product.

What is a diamond without pressure?

Remember the rough side is only a season. You'll make it to the summit.

God is working behind the scenes.

Search the Scriptures

One night I had a dream - I was in an old classroom with a blackboard and some wooden benches with people I didn't know. From what I could see or understand (as nothing was clear as day), we had an art workshop and another class after that.

There was a large canvas on a table easel, and on it was a seascape with a boat, but this boat was shaped like a guitar and as I was looking at it someone came and added a sail.

And something else stood out to me on the canvas but I didn't know what it was and why it was there.

After that there was a group discussion: someone asked my opinion on something and then we went back to our normal seats. The same person that asked my opinion said, "*How did you feel when I called on you?*" I said that it was a good thing and that I was challenged to communicate.

The latter part of the dream was easier to interpret but I felt led to search the scriptures, and God said to read Psalms. I was led to Psalm 92; it resonated with me but I needed more. So I looked for scriptures relating to stringed instruments and I was led to Habakkuk 3 (his prayer).

Habakkuk 3:19 (NKJV)
The Lord God is my strength; He will make my feet like deer's feet, And He will make me walk on my high hills. (*To the Chief Musician. With my stringed instruments.*)

The main themes throughout the short book of Habakkuk is struggle, doubt, God's Sovereignty and hope. He couldn't understand why a just God would allow such evil, and the wicked in Judah were not being punished. He doubted, he prayed and praised God for answering him.

Verse 19 encourages us and explains that;
- We should not doubt or be distressed by the events around us
- God gives us confidence in difficult times
- We must live in the strength of God's spirit
- God will bring about his justice
- In the long term, evil people will not prosper

God is alive and in control.

Note: The reference to the Chief musician/director was to be used when this passage was sung as a psalm in Temple worship.

God said he will give us a new song.

God isn't sovereign today and not sovereign the next. He is the same forevermore.

I encourage you all to believe in what we don't see. God is working behind the scenes.

Don't sit on your testimony.

Serve Your Testimony

Visualise yourself talking to a room of people or in a one-to-one capacity.

Who can you reach?

The one in the back who looks just like you. That person who might be going through what you went through. The one who may have their arms folded questioning why they're there, but by the power of your truth may set them free.

Luke 8:39 (NKJV)
"Return to your own house, and tell what great things God has done for you." And he went his way and proclaimed throughout the whole city what great things Jesus had done for him.

If you saw your old self in someone else, what would you tell them?

Don't sit on your testimony. Help someone who might be mentally starting to tap out, lose interest or lose hope. It will bring healing to them and yourself.

Stories are powerful and we all have something to share. They are personal and people attach themselves to authenticity.

I encourage you to reflect on the beauty of where you are today, how powerful you are and the influence you have.

Don't devalue you and remember your past is not your present or future! We have received a promise and are living, breathing, walking testimonies and there are so many more to come.

Rest in the assurance of God's Word and promise.

We are overcomers. We are conquerors.

Smarter than We Act

Life is cyclical; there are patterns all around us and within our individual lives.

Problems are also a part of these cycles. You may notice that you have been through something in the past and then it will rise up again. We can get addicted to our problems; we embody it. But we are not our problems. We are who God says we are.

Our minds get so attached to the problem and wanting to solve it. We're natural problem solvers, always seeking for a solution. The ultimate answer.

But we've been on certain roads before; we know that there is a hole in the road on a particular path but we keep walking that way. Each time the hole gets bigger and bigger, eventually taking us down. We have all the signs and warnings but yet we continue.

1 Peter 5:8 (NKJV)
Be sober, be vigilant; because your adversary the devil walks about like a roaring lion, seeking whom he may devour.

We're smarter than we act.

There are things we do and seek out for but only God can meet those needs. Sometimes God also allows these cycles and problems to happen to test us.

It's spiritual education; *have we really been educated? Have we really learnt that lesson?*

Only God can teach us the ultimate lesson to better ourselves; to enhance our spiritual development.

Psalm 16:11 (NKJV)
You will show me the path of life; In Your presence is fullness of joy; At Your right hand are pleasures forevermore.

Let's use our spiritual intelligence to rise above our problems and be conscious of our doings.

We are overcomers, we are conquerors.

There is peace in letting go.

Spiritual Senses

There are always parallels when it comes to our physical life and spiritual life, human form and spirit. Throughout different scriptures the Bible emphasizes the things that effect our senses, what we can do with our senses, and how we are blessed through our senses.

Here are some scriptures to mediate on where our spiritual senses are concerned.

Sight – "For we walk by faith, not by sight." (2 Corinthians 5:7 NKJV) This scripture encourages us not to focus on what we can see with our human eyes but to use our faith that we will be directed by God.
Hear – "So then faith comes by hearing, and hearing by the word of God. (Romans 10:17 NKJV)
Taste – "Oh, taste and see that the Lord is good; Blessed is the man who trusts in Him!" (Psalm 34:8 NKJV)
Smell – "For we are to God the fragrance of Christ among those who are being saved and among those who are perishing." (2 Corinthians 2:15 NKJV) How we offer our praise, worship, sacrifice and obedience.
Touch – "So Jesus had compassion and touched their eyes. And immediately their eyes received sight, and they followed Him." (Matthew 20:34 NKJV) We are blessed through God's touch of healing which is also a gift unto us that we can use towards others.

Our eyes, ears and mouth are our gateways that need to be guarded at all times. Another gate to consider is your heart. We can mediate and have a thought that becomes an action which then seeps into our heart. Someone may have done us wrong; we trick ourselves into believing that we have forgiven but, in our hearts, we still hold onto things – we hold grudges and the sound of someone's name still irritates us. There is peace in letting go; in the long term it hurts less to let go than to hold on. Wish them well.

Proverbs 4:20-27 (NKJV)

[20]My son, give attention to my words; Incline your ear to my sayings. [21]Do not let them depart from your eyes; Keep them in the midst of your heart; [22]For they are life to those who find them, And health to all their flesh. [23]Keep your heart with all diligence, For out of it spring the issues of life. [24]. Put away from you a deceitful mouth, And put perverse lips far from you. [25]Let your eyes look straight ahead, And your eyelids look right before you. [26]Ponder the path of your feet, And let all your ways be established. [27]. Do not turn to the right or the left; Remove your foot from evil.

Stay vigilant and walk in peace.

A legacy is built not bought!

The Grave is a Standard Size

Yes! I know the title sounds a bit morbid especially during this climate, but I can reassure you it's more of an emphasis on life rather than death.

We are not responsible for how we enter this world, but we are for how we leave. That span between life and death is the ultimate focus. The very essence of your existence, your purpose, your character, your energy, your story.

A legacy is built not bought!

Myles Munroe said, *"The greatest tragedy in life is not death, but a life without a purpose."*

We all have a purpose – as a matter of fact, everything under the sun was created for a purpose.

Those dreams and visions you once had and laid to rest – resurrect them! Make a start, give it a go! There is no harm in trying and it's even more amicable to start what you finished.

Anything is possible and opportunities are endless, but they don't fall onto our laps or knock on our doors. Opportunities may present themselves but sometimes we need to create them ourselves. There is room for you, there is room for your ideas, there is room for your master plans and the world needs you!

One thing I've learnt is that you shouldn't tell too many people your ideas. Yes, it's great to have one or two people for accountability purposes but you don't want to put it out to the wrong person and you don't receive the support you would like. Or risk the chance of not fulfilling what you said and that's not a good look.

Be a person of your word regardless – you owe it to yourself.

If you're someone like me who has a lot of ideas, I would advise that you pick one and execute that. Turn your goals into smaller ones – this allows for clarity and the smaller wins are just as important as the ultimate big win.

But it's not just about that BIG IDEA! - Purpose comes in many forms and is a combination of passion, talent, skills and abilities. Some of mine include creativity, giving advice, helping people and being empathetic. I don't take these for granted because I know the world around me needs these things. Never devalue the good seeds sown in your soul - you are someone's blessing.

Do you know your purpose? What are your goals?

How would you define your legacy? And what does that look like to you?

The answers may not come to you straight away and that's okay but make sure you take some time out for some well needed introspection - your future self will thank you for it. Remember this is yours and no one else's, so make it personal. There is no time like the present and in the words of my Dad - *Why put off what you can do today for tomorrow?*

Even in silence there is communication.

The Ultimate Key

Communication.

How we speak, write, through body language, how we love. Everything is communication! Even in silence there is communication.

Psalm 46:10 (NKJV)
Be still, and know that I am God; I will be exalted among the nations, I will be exalted in the earth!

Prayer, reading the Word and the Holy Spirit are the mightiest tools we have to communicate with God. Be attentive as God is speaking very loudly and clearly. God hears the echoes of our heart. God reflects and reveals His character to us. Through words, through dreams, through people.

May we not overcomplicate communication with God or ourselves. We should be understanding and full of compassion.

Ephesians 4:29-32 (NKJV)
[29]. Let no corrupt word proceed out of your mouth, but what is good for necessary edification, that it may impart grace to the hearers. [30]. And do not grieve the Holy Spirit of God, by whom you were sealed for the day of redemption. [31]. Let all bitterness, wrath, anger, clamor, and evil speaking be put away from you, with all malice. [32]. And be kind to one another, tenderhearted, forgiving one another, even as God in Christ forgave you.

If we are communicating privately or publicly onto God or one to another, may we use wisdom in response and attentiveness when hearing.

When uncertain be hopeful.

The Uncomfortable, Unexpected & Uncertainty

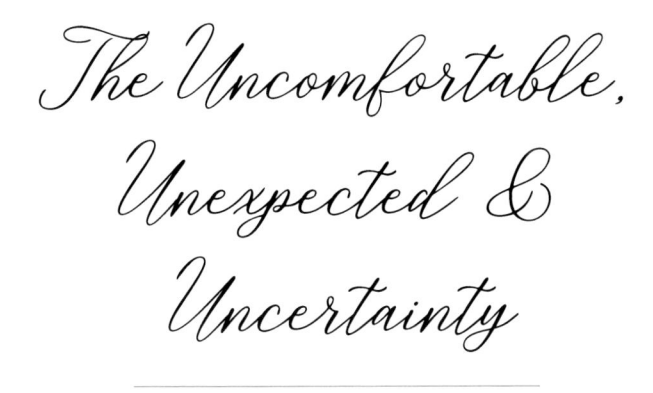

Comfortable in the uncomfortable
There are times when we have to do things that we don't want to do. It feels uncomfortable, but trust that all is well, and trust that you'll make or have made the right decisions. We have to learn to be comfortable in the uncomfortable. Uncomfortable allows for growth

God said he will do a new thing.

Isaiah 43:19 (NKJV)
Behold, I will do a new thing, Now it shall spring forth; Shall you not know it? I will even make a road in the wilderness And rivers in the desert.

Expect the unexpected
We may have a certain expectation of what we want to do, or what we expect or would like to happen. But things don't always pan out the way we want. Our timing is not God's timing. It doesn't always work our way because God has better in store for us. The unexpected allows us to change our perspective

Colossians 3:2 (NKJV)
Set your mind on things above, not on things on the earth.

When uncertain be hopeful
At times we may fear what is to come, due to uncertainty of the future. But the Word says;

Jeremiah 29:11 (NKJV)
For I know the thoughts that I think toward you, says the Lord, thoughts of peace and not of evil, to give you a future and a hope.

The value is in our own belief.

We are God's Masterpiece

Psalm 139:14 (KJV)
I will praise thee; for I am fearfully and wonderfully made: marvellous are thy works; and that my soul knoweth right well.

God has reminded me that we must look within and see ourselves how He sees us. To know who we are in Christ and that we have a purpose, we are worthy and are "a chosen generation, a Royal Priesthood" (1 Peter 2:9 NKJV).

Seeking validation from others will only bring about hurt and disappointment. The value is in our own belief. When you TRULY believe in who God says you are and walk in faith, you will have mastered peace.

Peace will reside because there is no conflict and no confusion but confidence.

Confidence that we know that we know that we know, and that we are sure and secure.

He has our backs in everything!

You are fearfully and wonderfully made and no-one can tell us otherwise.

Prayer + Practice
=
'Propertunity'

What Has Luck Got to do With it?

Absolutely nothing.

Proverbs 16:3 (KJV)
Commit thy works unto the Lord, and thy thoughts shall be established.

Opportunities come our way all the time, some by chance – things just happen. But we have a choice. Then some opportunities we have to seek after and pray about. We shouldn't just expect things to happen; we have to put in the work as well as being practical.

Prayer + Practice = 'Propertunity'
A proper opportunity

Being prayerful and practical will open doors. While you are being committed and consistent, you are planting seeds on good ground. God will protect and guide you. A reward awaits us all when God sees the fruits of our labor because we have put in the work while offering it unto him.

An addition to that is sacrifice and a type of sacrifice is fasting. Fasting is an element that allows our spirit to be more sensitive. Sacrificing to allow our spirits to be more sensitive to God's Spirit, we make room for divine spiritual food and a word.

In the midst of seeking our door of opportunity, we must also discern what is a good door and what is a bad door. Having our spirits levelled up to see good indicators will allow us to stop walking through the wrong door and being bruised unnecessarily.

While we may have the same level of excitement as someone who may feel lucky, we are blessed. And we can rejoice in God knowing that He made a way. **Go get your 'Propertunity'!**

Wisdom goes beyond just knowing but understanding.

Wisdom Has no age Restriction

Proverbs 9:9-12 (NKJV)
[9]. Give instruction to a wise man, and he will be still wiser; Teach a just man, and he will increase in learning. [10]. "The fear of the Lord is the beginning of wisdom, And the knowledge of the Holy One is understanding. [11]. For by me your days will be multiplied, And years of life will be added to you. [12]. If you are wise, you are wise for yourself, And if you scoff, you will bear it alone."

Wisdom goes beyond just knowing but understanding. Understanding through experience invites wise counsel.
Good wise counsel should hold no weight of judgement because we've been through certain experiences, we know how it feels; *who are we to judge?*

People will always have something to say, there will always be opinions, but we must sieve through the words.
There may be times when it may not come through someone, but direct nuggets of wisdom may drop in your spirit. Therefore, we must be sensitive to the voice of God and that is different to all of us.

Regardless of age, God will impart wisdom in all manner of things at different stages of our lives.

Wisdom allows for edification of oneself and for our fellow brothers and sisters.

We must always have a teachable spirit. Do not disregard someone's wisdom that we may not want to hear at that moment in time, but be receptive because that one thing might just change your life.

Each one, teach one.

Life is a journey

You and Yahweh

No-one is beneath you, and no-one is above you but God. We walk side by side with Jesus and when we can't walk, He carries us.

We have the authority and the audacity to access what is ours. We don't need to race against man to get where we need to be or want to. We must focus on God and not where others are. Comparing is not caring! Life is beautiful, life is a journey. No-one can live it for you.

But let's not take our inheritance for granted but move in authenticity and humility before God and be attentive to His voice.

May we not fear man, as man can do no eternal harm to us but fear God in reverence of His love and mercy towards us.

Proverbs 29:25 (NKJV)
The fear of man brings a snare, But whoever trusts in the Lord shall be safe.

Proclaim that you are royalty and you deserve riches.

Confess, trust and believe God.

Prayer

Heavenly Father, thank you for your grace and mercy. Bless your Holy name for you are great and worthy of all the honour and praise. Lord I pray for the person holding this book right now. I pray for your divine peace to be upon them always. I ask that whatever they seek, they will knock and you will answer. You know their hearts, you know the inner most parts that no one knows about, heal them from the inside out.

I pray that whatever fears have stopped them from pursuing their goals, dreams and visions, they will overcome, for you have given such talents. May they not bury them any longer but rise up and shine.

Lord I pray that they shall seek the wisdom of you and not lean on their own understanding and allow you to direct their paths. May their hearts not be troubled and Lord may your banner of love be over them.

Thank you for your everlasting love and when there seems to be no way, Lord you make a way. You are a true way maker and miracle worker.

I pray that they will practice speaking and thinking positively day to day and that their minds and hearts will be filled with such gratitude.

May they prosper in every area of their lives and live in hope.

I thank you for their lives. Bless them, cover them and protect them.

In Jesus name,
Amen.